$5 00

LOL
GOLF

———— • ————

by

Russ Edwards & Jack Kreismer

RED-LETTER PRESS, INC.
Saddle River, New Jersey

Red-Letter Press, Inc.
P.O. Box 393
Saddle River, NJ 07458

www.Red-LetterPress.com

ACKNOWLEDGMENTS

EDITORIAL:
Jeff Kreismer

•

BOOK DESIGN & TYPOGRAPHY:
Matt Taets

•

COVER & CONTENT ART:
Andrew Towl

•

PROJECT DEVELOPMENT:
Kobus Reyneke

Finally, this is to acknowledge that there will be no introduction since we are of the mindset that no one reads them, anyway. At the same time, in keeping with comedy legend Milton Berle's sentiments- "Laughter is an instant vacation"- we wish you a boatload of mini-trips with this LOL book.

–Jack Kreismer, Publisher

A thoroughly sloshed duffer stumbled into the nineteenth hole, staggered up to a woman at the bar and planted a big, wet, sloppy kiss right on her lips.

With that, the woman slapped him in the face and he came to his senses.

"Awfully sorry old girl," he said rubbing his cheek, "but you look exactly like my wife."

"You're a worthless, drunken, useless excuse for a human being," she snarled.

"Come to think of it," slurred the old inebriate, "you sound exactly like her too."

FORE!-HEAD

Mac McLendon wasn't doing very well in the first round of the 1979 Masters. He was possessed by an eerie feeling, that he was going to hit someone with one of his shots. That night he shared his fear with his wife Joan. A good and dutiful wife, she reassured him and gave him the confidence to go out the next day. Freed of his

> *"I learn English from American pros...*
> *That's why I speak so bad. I call it P.G.A. English."*
> **-Roberto de Vicenzo**

apprehensions, he knew he'd play better. On the first hole, with his very first swing, he managed to conk a spectator- his wife!

A couple of guys are standing around the water cooler Monday morning when one says, "What'd you do this weekend?"

"Dropped hooks in the water."

"Went fishing, eh?"

"No, golfing."

A pair of duffers are waiting their turn on the tee, when a drop-dead gorgeous woman in her birthday suit runs across the fairway and into the woods. Two men in white coats and another guy carrying two buckets of sand are chasing after her, and a little old man is bringing up the rear.

"What the heck is going on here?" one of the golfers asks the old geezer.

> *"Retire to what? I'm a golfer and a fisherman.*
> *I've got no place to retire to."*
> **-Julius Boros**

He says, "She's a nymphomaniac from the funny farm. She keeps escaping from the asylum and us attendants are trying to catch her."

The golfer says, "What about that guy with the buckets of sand?"

"Oh, him. That's his handicap. He caught her last time."

BAR FOR THE COURSE

Back in 1974, during an Amateur Stroke Play event, Nigel Denham hit his second shot right into the clubhouse, winding up in the men's bar. As it wasn't out of bounds, Nigel opened a window and sent the ball to the green, landing just twelve feet from the hole.

Doctor Dudley, toting his golf bag, was heading out of his dentist's office when his receptionist said, "Doctor, I have Mr. Arnold on the line. He has a toothache."

Dudley answered, "Tell him to call back tomorrow. I've got eighteen cavities to fill today."

> *"Being left-handed is a big advantage: no one knows enough about your swing to mess you up with advice."*
> **-Bob Charles**

A golfer sliced his ball right off the course, hitting a lawyer who was walking down a nearby sidewalk.

The golfer ran over to the stricken lawyer to see if he was all right. "Im going to sue you for five thousand dollars," the lawyer said.

"I'm awfully sorry but I yelled 'Fore!'"

"I'll take it!" the lawyer replied.

A panic-stricken golfer charged into the clubhouse, grabbed the pro by the arm and said, "You gotta help! I was on the ninth hole and hit a terrible slice. The ball sailed right off the course and hit a guy riding a motorcycle. He lost control and swerved into the path of a truck. The truck tried to stop but jack-knifed, rolled over and broke apart. It was carrying thousands of bee hives and now the bees are attacking everyone in sight. It's awful! It's a disaster! What should I do?"

The pro answered, "Well, the first thing is you've got to keep your arms straight and remember to get your right hand a bit more under the club ..."

WHAT'S IT CALLED WHEN YOU PURCHASE A SET OF CLUBS AT LIST PRICE?

WHITE HOUSE WOES

First Birthers, then Deathers and now Golfers. It seems in some quarters, President Barack Obama can't get no respect. The first African-American president and the first sitting president in 90 years to win a Nobel Prize is now BadGolfer.com's first Bad Golfer of the Decade in the 21st century. According to them, Obama apparently stinks on the links.

In the good old days, you could always rely on seeing President Eisenhower in cool-headed command out on the course or President Clinton happily playing a round. Obama is more like President Jerry Ford, where his secret service men had to be willing to "take a golf ball for the President". While Jerry spent most of his time in sand traps, the spectators spent most of theirs in a bunker- the bullet-proof kind. Obama hasn't yet launched any dimpled missiles of mass destruction on the golf course as of this writing, but when the First Duffer steps out of Golf Cart One, we know his handicap is in the 20's. According to *Golf Digest*, "Obama's golf game is not good."

To sum up the opinion of golf writers everywhere, Obama is a man of the people- people who can't really play golf.

GETTING SHAFTED

The drill sergeant decides to play a late afternoon-early evening game of golf and hooks up to play a twosome.

Four quadruple bogeys, three triple bogeys and two double bogeys later the sarge's partner says, "When did you take up this game?"

The drill sergeant says, "Nineteen fifty-nine."

"Nineteen fifty-nine?" says the other golfer. "I would think that you'd be able to play a little better than this."

"Whaddya mean?" says the sarge. "It's only twenty-two thirteen right now."

A duffer sliced his tee shot right into the woods. Rather than take a penalty, he decided to go for it. Unfortunately, his second shot caromed right off the trunk of a big old oak tree, hitting him right between the eyes and killing him instantly.

The next thing he knew, he was standing before St. Peter at the Pearly Gates.

St. Peter, trying to find his name on the list, said, "Oh, here it is. But according to this, you're not scheduled to die for another 25 years. How did you get here?"

"In two."

THOUGHTS OF THE THRONE

Lee Trevino, talking of the similar roots he and Seve Ballesteros share, once said, "We come from the same backgrounds, more or less, where growing up next to a golf course didn't mean a 10,000-square foot house and gold faucets in the bathroom."

• • •

While SuperMex was on the PGA tour in 1968, he visited The Alamo, in San Antonio, Texas. Trevino was heard to say, "Well, I'm not gonna buy this place. It doesn't have indoor plumbing."

• • •

An exhausted Fuzzy Zoeller, after 36 holes on the final rain-delayed day of the 1981 Colonial National Invitation tournament said, "It was a very long day. I don't know how long we've been out there, but I know it's time to shave again."

• • •

When golfer Johnny Pott was introduced at the Los Angeles Open in the 1960s, the announcer committed this blooper: "Now on the pot, Johnny Tee."

"I dreamed I made 17 holes-in-one, and then on the 18th hole I lipped the cup and I was madder than hell."
-Ben Hogan

Joyce Kasmierski, on network television at the 1983 Women's Kemper Open, said this about weather conditions: "The wind was so strong there were whitecaps in the porta-john."

• • •

Dave Stockton, complaining of the difficulty of playing Poppy Hills Golf Course in Pebble Beach, California, was heard to say, "Even the men's room has a double dogleg."

A golfer goes to a psychiatrist and says, "My wife thinks I'm crazy because I like plaid golf socks."

"That's not so strange," says the doc. "I kind of like them, too."

"Really?" exclaimed the patient, excited to find a sympathetic ear. "Do you like yours with chocolate fudge or Hollandaise sauce?"

• • •

A politician died and, as might be expected, he went straight to Hell. As Satan was showing him around the place, he noticed a beautiful golf course that would put Augusta to shame. Being a lifelong golf fanatic, he was thrilled. Striding into the pro shop, he

> *"Golf practice: something you do to convert a nasty hook into a wicked slice."*
> **-Henry Beard**

spotted a sign that read, "Only the Finest Equipment and All Absolutely Free – Help Yourself."

Having selected a fantastic set of matched clubs and a first class golf bag, he next needed a caddy. The caddy shack was filled with gorgeous women who were movie stars in life. He chose Marilyn Monroe, who was wearing a teddy. He couldn't wait to begin his dream game! As he stepped up to the tee, he reached into the ball pocket and found it empty. He looked up to see Satan grinning from ear to ear.

"Don't bother going back to the pro shop. There aren't any balls anywhere – You see, that's the Hell of it."

A duffer walks into the nineteenth hole, orders three stiff ones and downs them immediately, then starts sobbing uncontrollably. The bartender says, "Hey, buddy, calm down. What's the matter?"

"My wife just left me for my golfing partner," he sobs.

"That's okay. Take it easy. There are plenty of other fish in the sea," says the bartender.

"I'm not worried about that," the duffer cries, "but he's the only one I could ever beat."

> *"In golf, I'm one under- one under a tree, one under a rock, and one under a bush."*
> **-Gerry Cheevers**

A guy has been stranded on an island for ages. One day as he's walking on the beach, a beautiful woman in a wet suit emerges from the surf.

"Hey, cutie pie. Have you been here long?" she asks.

"I reckon about ten years."

"Do you smoke?"

"Oh, what I'd do for a cigarette!" he responds. With that, she unzips a pocket in the sleeve of her wet suit, pulls out a pack of cigarettes, lights one and gives it to him.

"I guess it's been a long while since you've had a drink, huh?"

"You got that right," he says. She pulls out a flask from another pocket, gives it to him and he takes a swig.

"I bet you haven't played around in a while either," she coos as she begins to unzip the front of her wet suit.

Wide-eyed, he says, "Don't tell me you have a set of golf clubs in there too!?"

WHAT DO PEDIATRICIANS PLAY ON WEDNESDAYS?

DUFFER'S DEAREST

The first woman to write a book about golf was Mrs. Edward Kennard. In 1896, she penned the text which was titled *The Sorrows of a Golfer's Wife*.

EXPENSIVE TRIP

At the 1988 Canadian Open, Dave Bally had an easy putt, but as he approached his ball, he tripped, sending his putter flying into the ball and knocking it off the green into a nearby pond. He wound up with a triple bogey on the par three hole.

On a blistering day in south Florida, a priest, a minister and a rabbi were playing golf alongside beautiful Biscayne Bay. As the mercury climbed past 90, 95 and then topped 100 degrees, the men of cloth couldn't take it any longer. The bay looked so inviting that they decided to strip down and jump in the water.

MINIATURE GOLF

After frolicking and splashing about for a while, they figured that they'd cooled down enough to get back to their game.

Before they could dress, a foursome of lady golfers appeared nearby. The minister and priest covered their private parts in a panic, but the rabbi just covered his face. After the women passed by, the priest and minister asked the rabbi why he covered his face instead of his privates.

As the rabbi fastened the last button to his shirt, he replied, "Listen, I don't know about you, but in my congregation it's the face they'll recognize."

Rex had a particularly bad day on the course. Nothing went right, and by the time he missed a two-foot putt on the 17th to round his score up to 130, he blew his stack.

He removed his golf clubs from his bag and cracked them over his knees before hurling them into the water.

"I'll never play golf again," he roared. He then kicked the bag around, tossed that in the water too, and in a super-human burst

"Tee up the ball high — air offers less resistance than dirt."
-Jack Nicklaus

of rage, flipped the golf cart over into the lake. At that point, he stomped off toward the clubhouse.

One of the members happened by, just missing the tantrum, and innocently asked, "Hey Rex, we need a fourth for tomorrow. Can you make it?"

Rex stopped in his tracks, looked up and said, "What time?"

Harry loved golf more than anything, but as he got into his 80's his eyesight began to fail him.

Commiserating about his problem at the nineteenth hole, he met Louie, another octogenarian who lived for golf and, although he had perfect eyesight, was crippled by arthritis. They decided to join forces and play a round the next morning. Harry teed off and the ball hooked a wee bit but landed not too far left of the green.

"Hey, that felt good, Louie. Did you see where the ball went?"

"Sure did," replied Louie.

"So where'd it land?"

Louie scratched his head and replied, "I forget."

GOLF AS AN INDOOR SPORT

Former Detroit Lions football player Alex Karras once hit a ball
through a dining room window at the club where he was playing.
Karras calmly walked over to the groundskeeper and asked, "Is this
room out of bounds?"

The Sheik of all sheiks was rushed to the hospital for an emergency
appendectomy. The attending surgeon expertly removed the organ
without serious complications.

"You saved my life," said the Sheik upon regaining consciousness.
"Anything you want is yours."

"That's not necessary," responded the doctor.

"But I insist," said the Sheik.

"Well, okay, I could use a new set of matched clubs."

"Done!" said the Sheik.

A few weeks went by and the busy doctor had forgotten all about
the Sheik's promise when a fax arrived. It read:

From: The Sheik
To: The Good Doctor
I have bought you the new set of golf clubs you requested, but am
eternally embarrassed and humbled that they sadly do not match. I was
appalled to discover that four do not have swimming pools.

An executive who often left to play golf during business hours told his secretary to advise all callers that he was away from his desk. A golfer who was part of the executive's foursome forgot where they were playing on one particular day, so he called the secretary. Loyal to a fault, she'd only say that her boss was away from his desk.

Finally, the exasperated golfer said, "Look, just tell me. Is he five miles or ten miles away from his desk?"

DRIVE TIME

Here's what they have to say about driving with John Daly:

"His driving is unbelievable. I don't go that far on my holidays." -Ian Baker-Finch

"Did you know John Daly hit a tee shot – and two tracking stations picked it up as a satellite?" -Jim Murray

"He is just ridiculous with his length. I couldn't hit it where he hits it on a runway." -Fred Funk

"Hazards attract – fairways repel."
-Anonymous

A small private plane was flying over southwest Florida when all of a sudden the engine died, miles away from any airport. The pilot turned to his wife and said, "Don't worry honey, there are dozens of golf courses in this area. I'll just land on the next one I see."

To which his wife replied, "What do you mean 'don't worry'? I've seen you play. You'll never hit the fairway!"

SOMETIMES YOU JUST CAN'T WIN

In 1982, John Murphy went out to play a quiet round of golf by himself in Raleigh, North Carolina. To his amazement he aced the fifth hole, but because he was alone, it wasn't official. After the game, Murphy led the assistant greenskeeper back to the fifth hole, teed up and repeated the hole-in-one. Sadly, as it wasn't scored during an official round, that one didn't count either.

HOW CAN YOU SPOT THE GOLFERS IN CHURCH?

A very prominent CEO of a very big company was sent this ransom message: "If you ever want to see your wife again, bring $100,000 to the 16th green of Deerfield at eleven o'clock sharp tomorrow."

Well, the CEO didn't get there until noon. A masked man jumped out from behind some bushes and snarled, "What took you so long? You're an hour late."

"Hey, cut me some slack," said the CEO. "I have a twenty-five handicap."

NICE SHOT

Golfer Bob Russell took a practice shot on a municipal course in Ohio in 1974 and felt a terrible pain in his leg. The head of his driver hit a bullet that someone had carelessly left behind. Fortunately, the wound was minor- although it did ruin a perfectly good pair of golf pants.

Fred, playing as a single, was teamed with a twosome. Eventually, they asked why he was playing by himself on such a beautiful day.

THEY'RE THE ONES WHO PRAY WITH THE
INTERLOCKING GRIP.

"My dear wife and I played this course together for over thirty years, but this year she passed away. I kept the tee time in her memory."

The twosome were touched at the thoughtfulness of the gesture, but one asked him why no one from among her friends and family was willing to take her spot.

"Oh," responded Fred, "they're all at the funeral."

A minister and his very conservative wife had a great marriage, except for his long business trips and lifelong obsession with golf.

One day while he was away, she was cleaning and found a box of mementos in the back of the bedroom closet. In it she found three golf balls and $800.

That night when he called, she asked him the meaning of the three golf balls. He said, "Well dear, I've been keeping that box for twenty years. I'm ashamed to admit it, but so great is my passion for the game of golf that occasionally I swear on the course. Every

"When you look up and hit an awful shot, you will always look down again at exactly the moment you ought to start watching the ball — if you ever want to see it again."
-Henry Beard

time I use unsavory language, I penalize myself one golf ball."

Shocked that her husband, a man of the cloth, would ever use four-letter words, the wife was at first taken aback but then thought, "Well, three balls means that he's only cursed three times in 20 years. I suppose that isn't so bad."

"All right dear," she said, "I forgive you for your lapses, but tell me, what's the $800 for?"

"Oh that," answered the minister. "I found a guy who buys golf balls at two bucks a dozen."

SENIOR SENTIMENTS

"You know this is the Senior Tour when your back goes out more than you do."
-Bob Bruce

"When you get up there in years, the fairways get longer and the holes get smaller."
-Bobby Locke

"If you need to ask your caddy for advice, he should be hitting the shots and you carrying the bag."
-Lee Trevino

*"Reporters used to ask me questions about the condition of my game.
Now all they ask about is the condition of my health."*
-Jack Nicklaus

*"It's like getting divorced and getting remarried
the same morning."*
**-Jay Sigel, on becoming 50 and giving up his amateur status to
play on the Senior Tour**

"It's a grind trying to beat 60-year-old kids out there."
**-Sam Snead, explaining why he quit
playing on the Senior Tour at age 77**

"What's nice about our tour is you can't remember your bad shots."
-Bob Bruce

"Combination rest home and gold mine."
-Dan Jenkins, about the Senior Tour

*"Golf is the one game I know which becomes more and more
difficult the longer one plays it."*
-Bobby Jones

At a hoity toity country club, a member saw a guest of the club place his ball five inches in front of the tee markers. The member ran over to the guest and said, "Sir, I don't know whether you've ever played here before, but we have very stringent rules about placing your tee at or behind the markers before driving the ball."

The guest looked the snooty club member right in the eye and retorted, "First, I've never played here before. Second, I don't care about your rules. And third, this is my second shot."

• • •

A husband and wife, both golf fanatics, were discussing the future as they sat by a warm fireplace. "Dear," the wife said, "if I died, would you remarry?"

"Well, I imagine so... After all, we're not exactly senior citizens."

"Would you live in this house with her?" the wife asked.

"I would think so."

She continued, "How about my car? Would she get that?"

"I don't see why not."

"What about my golf clubs? Would you give them to her too?"

"Heck, no," the husband exclaimed. "She's left-handed."

"Only on days ending in 'y'."
**-Jerry West, when asked how often he would play golf
after retiring from basketball**

A lawyer mailed a note to his client:
"Dear Mr. Foxworth: Thought I saw you at the nineteenth hole yesterday... Went over to your table to say hello, but it wasn't you so I went back. One twentieth of an hour: $20."

A terrible golfer hits a ball into a gigantic bunker. He asks his caddy, "What club should I use now?"

The caddy says, "The club isn't the important thing. Just make sure to take along plenty of food and water."

SLICE-PRESIDENT

Though Gerald Ford is famed for his golfing mishaps, former Vice President Spiro Agnew also racked up an impressive body count. On February 13, 1971 Agnew hit a husband and wife with just one shot. On his next swing, he took out a woman spectator by bopping

WHAT DO HACKERS AND CONDEMNED PLAYGROUNDS HAVE IN COMMON?

her on the ankle. Since he was thoroughly warmed up, he went out the next day and cracked Doug Sanders in the noggin. Bob Hope said of Agnew, "He can't cheat on his scorecard. All you have to do to find out the number of strokes he took is look down the fairway and count the bodies."

PRESIDENTIAL PESTS

Richard Nixon may have had bugs and leaks, but Dwight Eisenhower had a squirrel problem at the White House. The frisky critters were interfering with his putting practice on the lawn, so he ordered them trapped and taken elsewhere. It wasn't as humane as you'd think. After all, where else but Washington, D.C. were the squirrels going to find as many nuts?

Did you hear the one about the pub for vulgar golfers? It's called Par for the Coarse.

LOUSY SWINGS

Goldfarb died and left no family, but he did leave dozens of golfing buddies. At the service, Schaffer, one of his best friends, came up to the coffin and placed an envelope full of cash in it.

"Goldie, I've owed you this thousand dollars far too long. I wanted to make sure I paid off my golfing bet."

A few moments later, Anderson, another golf crony, placed an envelope of cash in the coffin and said, "Here's that golf bet payoff from last summer. Now we're even."

Later on, after everyone had been to the cemetery, the guys decided to hoist a few in Goldfarb's memory at the nineteenth hole. At one point, Schaffer and Anderson approached McCoy, who, by that time, was feeling no pain.

"We were wondering," said Schaffer, "did you get around to paying Goldfarb that $1,500 you owed him?"

"I certainly did," replied McCoy. "When I went up to the casket, I put it in."

"That was decent of you," said Anderson. "That coffin certainly had an awful lot of money in it."

"Golf is the most human game of all. You have the same highs and lows — sometimes in the same round."
-Lee Trevino

"That concerned me too," said McCoy. "That's why, when I went up there, I took out the envelopes that had $2,000 in them and threw in a check for $3,500."

A terribly slow-playing golfer was getting heat from his caddy all afternoon when he finally lost his cool. "I've had enough of your snide remarks. When we get back to the clubhouse, I'll see that you no longer have any work here."

"You gotta be kidding," said the caddy. "By the time we get there, I'll be retired."

DIRTY POOL

At the first Amateur Championship in 1895, the USGA ruled that Richard Peters would not be able to use his trusty putter – a pool cue.

"Never wash your ball on the tee of a water hole."
-Mulligan's Laws

Maybe you've heard why clergymen play such poor golf... They don't have the vocabulary for it.

Arnold Palmer and Tiger Woods were playing the fourteenth hole when Tiger's tee shot landed behind a huge 75-foot sycamore tree. Tiger looked at Arnie and said, "How would you play this one? Lay up and take an extra stroke?"

Arnie replied, "When I was your age, I'd just play right over the tree."

Tiger, not wanting to be shown up by the old master, proceeded to hit the ball high, but not high enough. It bounced off the tree and dropped out of bounds. Tiger, really ticked at this point, asked, "Arnie, how did you ever hit a ball over that tree?"

Arnie replied, "Well, when I was your age, that tree was only three feet tall."

> *"The secret of missing a tree is to aim straight at it."*
> **-Michael Green**

A retiree was given a set of golf clubs by his co-workers. Thinking he'd try the game, he asked the local pro for lessons, explaining that he knew nothing whatever of the sport.

The pro showed him the stance and swing, then said, "Just hit the ball toward the flag on the first green."

The novice teed up and smacked the ball straight down the fairway and onto the green, where it stopped inches from the hole.

"Now what?" the fellow asked the speechless pro.

After he was able to speak again, the pro finally said, "Uh, you're supposed to hit the ball into the cup."

The beginner responded, "Oh, great! Now you tell me!"

Four old duffers had a Saturday morning 8 o'clock tee time for years. On one such morning, they noticed a guy watching them as they teed off. At every tee, he caught up with them and had to wait. When they reached the fifth tee, the guy walked up to the foursome and handed them a card which read, "I am deaf and mute. May I play through?"

> *"If you have a bad grip, you don't want a good swing."*
> **-Harvey Penick**

The old duffers were outraged, and signaled to him that nobody plays through their group. He'd just have to bide his time.

On the eighth hole, one of the foursome was in the fairway lining up his second shot. All of the sudden, he got bopped in the back of the head by the tremendous force of a golf ball. He turned around and looked back at the tee. There stood the deaf mute, frantically waving his arm in the air, holding up four fingers.

A real fire-and-brimstone fundamentalist preacher always made it a point to admonish his flock about playing golf on the Sabbath. But, alas, one springtime Sunday morning, the preacher himself was tempted to play a quick round. Up in Heaven, the angel in charge of such things, Melrose, spotted the minister and was outraged at his hypocrisy. Melrose went to see the Big Guy and told him of the reverend's transgression.

"I agree he should be punished," said God. "I'll take care of it."

HOW IS A WEDDING RING LIKE A BAG OF GOLF CLUBS?

With that, back down on the course, the preacher stepped up to the tee and hit the ball perfectly. It sailed down the fairway, cleared all the hazards, plopped down on the green and rolled gently into the cup for an ace. Melrose was flabbergasted. "A hole-in-one? I thought you were going to punish him."

"I did," God replied. "Who's he going to tell?"

A golf club walks into a bar and asks for a beer. The bartender refuses to serve him.

"Why not?" demands the golf club.

"Because you'll be driving later."

• • •

Phone conversation at the nineteenth hole: "Hello, Fairleigh Golf Club. I'd like to find out if my husband is there."

"No ma'am."

"You haven't even heard my name. How can you possibly know he isn't there?"

"Because ma'am, no husband is ever here when his wife calls."

THEY ARE BOTH INSTRUMENTS OF ETERNAL SERVITUDE.

GRAVE CONSEQUENCES

Because the golf course in Tientsin, China is laid out in a cemetery, greens are situated between grave mounds. Local rule: A ball which rolls into an open grave may be lifted without penalty.

Old Findley finally went to that big golf course in the sky, leaving an estate of $200,000. After all his final expenses were paid at the funeral home, his widow confided to her closest friend that there was nothing left.

"Nothing?" the woman asked incredulously. "How can that be? You said he had $200,000."

"Well," replied the widow Findley, "the funeral cost $8,000 and there was the matter of $2,000 back dues at the country club. The rest went for the memorial stone."

"$190,000 for a memorial stone?! That's unbelievable. How big was it?"

The widow smiled and sighed, "Oh, just over seven carats."

Hank the hack was having his usual day on the links, hitting into the woods, losing balls and, in general, making his caddy's job horrible. On the fifteenth, he approached the ball on the fairway and hollered at the caddy to give him a three-wood.

"Uh, excuse me," the caddy began to say.

"Just be quiet and give me the three-wood," Hank demanded.
The caddy gave it to him and watched. Hank then hit a beautiful shot
that bounced once on the fairway, then onto the green and into the
cup for a 1 under. "You see that," said Hank, "I know what I'm doin',
kid."

"Heckuva shot, sir," said the exasperated caddy. "It's just a shame it
wasn't your ball."

• • •

Waiting to tee off, an Atlanta gentleman spotted a funeral
procession going down a nearby road. It was led by a man walking
a dog, followed by the hearse and about 75 to 80 men in single
file. As they passed by, the golfer bowed his head and then asked
the man about the strange procession.

"Well, suh," drawled the man, "you see, this is my wife's funeral
and she died because this dog bit her."

"I'm terribly sorry for your loss," responded the golfer, "but
would you mind if I borrowed the dog for a while?"

"Sure," said the widower, "get in the back of the line."

> *"The devoted golfer is an anguished soul who has
> learned a lot about putting just as an avalanche victim
> has learned a lot about snow."*
> **-Dan Jenkins**

A MATTER OF COURSE

Golf was banned in England in 1457 because it was considered a distraction from the useful pursuit of archery. It is true that in archery you usually make a hole with one shot.

Two old buddies were out on the links on a scorching Wednesday afternoon. On the fifth hole, the first old duffer collapses right on the green. His buddy shouts for help. A pair of doctors playing the fourth hole quickly drive their cart over. One takes out his emergency kit, examines the old guy and says, "I'm sorry, but your friend is dead."

"He was in perfect condition," said the oldster. "That just can't be. I want a second opinion."

With that, the second doctor goes back to his cart, takes out a small cat from his golf bag, and places it near the dead man. The cat sniffs around the man's feet, walks around his body sniffing all the while, and then sits down and begins meowing at the doctor.

"What's that supposed to mean?" asks the old duffer.

"If every golfer in the world, male and female, were laid end to end, I for one, would leave them there."
-Mark Parkinson, President of the Anti-Golf Society

"The cat says your friend is dead," responds the doctor.

The man tearfully says, "I can't believe it."

"That'll be three hundred fifty dollars," says the doctor.

"What? I would agree to pay something, but where do you get off charging me three hundred fifty bucks?"

"It's fifty dollars for the diagnosis," replies the doctor, "and three hundred dollars for the cat scan."

BRIEF STORY

John Daly made the news when he inked a 2010 sponsorship deal to prance around in Slix underwear, but way back when, "brief" talk was rarely for public discourse. That's why the folks at the Hillcrest Country Club in Beverly Hills once considered revoking the memberships of comedians George Burns and Harpo Marx. The reason - they played a round of golf in their whitey tighties.

> *"Golf is great exercise, particularly climbing in
> and out of the carts."*
> **-Jack Berry**

Two old golfers were reminiscing as they played. One pointed towards the woods. "My first girlfriend was named Mary Katherine Agnes Colleen Patricia Marion Margaret Kathleen O'Shaugnessey. Back when I was a lad, working as a caddy, I carved her name in one of those trees right over there."

"Whatever happened?" asked his friend.

"The tree fell on me."

A guy went to a psychiatrist and announced, "There's nothing wrong with me, Doc, but my wife says if I don't come see you, she's getting a divorce."

"And exactly what does she think is the matter?" asked the shrink.

"Well," the new patient replied, "you see, I'm Jack Nicklaus and she seems to think there's something wrong with that."

A bit surprised, the psychiatrist asked, "Jack Nicklaus, as in the world-famous golfer?"

WHAT ARE THE FOUR WORST WORDS YOU COULD HEAR DURING A GAME OF GOLF?

"Yep, that's me."

Knowing full well that the patient sitting before him was not Jack Nicklaus, the doctor prescribed three therapy sessions a week. After two years of this intensive treatment, the psychiatrist announced to his patient, "Congratulations, you're cured."

"Congratulations for what?" grumbled his patient. "Before I came to you, I was Jack Nicklaus. Now I'm a nobody."

WHO'S THE REAL GOAT HERE?

At Florida's Sawgrass, Pete Dye got the idea to keep the weedy undergrowth in the rough under control by using small herds of goats as they do in Ireland. The idea worked for a short time and then they had to buy mowers. Pete forgot that Ireland doesn't have alligators.

"IT'S STILL YOUR TURN!"

A guy walks into the 19th Hole and orders two martinis. The bartender serves them and says, "If it's all the same to you, buddy, I could have made a double and used one glass."

The guy says, "Oh, I know, but my golfing partner died and, just before he did, I promised him I'd order him a drink after each round of golf."

The next week the guy comes back and says to the bartender, "I'll have a martini."

The bartender says, "And one for your buddy, too?"

He says, "Oh, no. This is for my buddy. I'm on the wagon."

A duffer made a terrible shot and, in the process, tore up a gigantic piece of turf. He picked it up, turned to his caddy and said, "What should I do with it?"

The caddy replied, "If I were you, I'd take it home to practice on."

> *"It matters not the sacrifice which makes the duffer's wife so sore. I am the captive of my slice. I am the servant of my score."*
> **-Grantland Rice**

At his 50th wedding anniversary party held at the local country club, Grandpa Steve was asked the secret of his long marriage. He stood up before his assembled crowd of friends and relatives and shared his marital philosophy.

"Gertrude and I have made it a practice throughout our long marriage to play golf and then go out for two romantic, candlelit dinners a week - right here at this country club. Unfailingly, twice a week, we come here and enjoy the delicious food and soft music. We soak up the ambiance of this fine establishment and sip a vintage wine. She goes Thursdays and I go Fridays."

Old Cornwaithe was playing alone at Pebble Beach one foggy day when he heard a voice from the nearby water hazard.

"Hey, Mister," the voice said.

He looked around but saw no one, so he resumed his slow creak towards the green.

"The smaller the ball used in the sport, the better the book."
-George Plimpton, explaining why books on golf and baseball are better than those about football and basketball

A few seconds later, he heard, "Hey, Mister," once again.

He parted the tall grass at the edge of the water and looked down at a frog perched on a leaf.

The frog said, "Yeah, it's me."

"So what do you want, frog?" the old man wheezed.

"Listen, Mister," the frog replied. "I'm really a beautiful princess, but an evil witch has cast a spell upon me and turned me into an ugly, slimy frog. All I need is a kiss and I'll turn back into a gorgeous princess. Pick me up, kiss me and then I'm all yours."

With that, the old man scooped up the frog and slipped her in his golf bag.

"Hey, Mister," the frog protested. "Aren't you going to kiss me? What about all the fun you can have with me?"

"Thanks just the same," Cornwaithe responded, "but at my age, I'd just as soon have a talking frog."

And then there was the guy whose doctor advised him to play 36 holes a day so he went out and bought a harmonica.

"Isn't it fun to go out on the course and lie in the sun?"
-Bob Hope

FUHGEDDABOUDIT!

At the 1990 Australian Open, Brett Ogle had his kneecap broken by his ball after it deflected off a tree.

• • •

Gary Player was on his way to defending his Masters championship in 1962 when an overzealous fan with an iron grip shook his hand and sprained it. Player was forced to play the final round with a bandaged hand and eventually lost a play-off to Arnold Palmer.

• • •

Lee Trevino was leading the final round of the 1970 British Open by three strokes, but pulled a colossal boner on the fifth hole when he hit the ball to the wrong stick. He never recovered and Jack Nicklaus wound up winning the tournament.

• • •

Bob Rosburg missed a three-foot putt on the seventy-second hole to lose the U.S. Open by one stroke to Orville Moody.

"Be funny on a golf course? Do I kid my best friend's mother about her heart condition?"
-Phil Silvers

By the time a man can afford to lose a golf ball, he can't hit that far.

A guy runs into the pro shop and yells, "Quick. Do you know a cure for a terrible case of hiccups?"

Without saying a word, the pro gives the guy a swift kick to the stomach, forcing him to gasp for air.

"I bet you don't have the hiccups now," says the pro.

"No, but my partner on the first tee does."

A man went to a therapist for a consultation about an obsession that was ruining his health. "It's golf, Doc. Golf is destroying me. I'm desperate. I can't even escape it in my sleep. As soon as I close my eyes, I'm out there sinking a two-foot putt or making a magnificent drive right down the fairway. When I wake up in the

WHAT'S THE DEFINITION OF A MULLIGAN?

morning, I'm even more tired than I was before I went to bed. What am I going to do? Can you help me?"

The therapist answered reassuringly, "First of all, you are going to have to make a conscious effort not to dream about golf. For example, when you close your eyes at night, try to imagine something else exciting, like discovering a gold mine or sailing on an around-the-world cruise."

The patient replied, "That's easy for you to say, Doc. If I do that, I'll miss my tee-time."

The newcomer to the course was studying the ball and its distance from the green. "What do you think?" he asked the caddy.

"Well, yesterday I caddied for Ray Romano. He hits 'em about like you. I advised him to use an eight-iron."

With that, the golfer took out his eight-iron, addressed the ball and played his shot- a shot that fell far short of the green.

The angry golfer said, "I thought you told Ray Romano to use an eight."

"I did. He didn't reach the green either."

THE OPPORTUNITY TO REPEAT A MISTAKE
RIGHT AWAY

"Father," the young man said to the priest, "Is it a sin to play golf on Christmas Day?"

"My son," replied the padre, placing his hand on the fellow's shoulder, "The way you play golf, it's a sin any day."

Charlie showed up for an early tee time looking exhausted.

"Hey Charlie, what happened?" asked his golfing buddy.

"Oh, I had a big fight with my wife," he replied, still a bit dazed.

"I thought your wife was out of town last night."

"Yeah," Charlie answered ruefully. "So did I."

Harry was playing a short hole when his drive smacked into a bird, which fell right into the cup. This marked the first time ever for a partridge in a par three.

"Learning to play golf is like learning to play the violin. It's not only difficult, it's very painful to everyone around you."
-Hal Linden

Two guys were at the nineteenth hole discussing their golf game. "This is one heckuva tough course to play," said one of them. "How did you do?"

"Oh, pretty much the same as I always do," replied the second duffer. "I'm a pre-putt-par."

"What's that mean?" asked the other guy.

"It means I shoot par on the fairway and four- putt on the green."

HITTING SPECTATORS IS EASY, SHOOTING DOWN A PLANE IS HARD

In Livermore, California, a golfer who got a bit too much loft managed to send his ball through the windshield of a small plane in the process of landing at a nearby airport. Although the pilot took a terrific crack to the noggin, the plane touched down safely, which goes to prove that flying is safer than driving.

"Dams and lakes are sacrificial waters where you make a steady gift of your pride and high-priced balls."
-Tommy Bolt

Jed Clampett: "We're gonna be shooting some game called golf."

Granny: "What in tarnation is that?"

Jed: "I don't know, but they sure must be thicker'n crows in a corn patch around here because everybody in Beverly Hills shoots 'em."

Granny: "Never seen 'em around. They must live in holes in the ground like a gopher."

Jed: "Reckon maybe you're right. Mr. Drysdale says he shot nine holes of golf and got fifty-seven."

-From *The Beverly Hillbillies*

POLO GOLF

The Polo Golf Derby, played in Hempstead, Long Island, is for golfers and their carts. Players may only leave their carts while putting. It's all about hitting the ball without slowing down. The fastest time and the fewest strokes wins. Talk about being a good driver!

"I owe a lot to my parents, especially my mother and father."
-Greg Norman

MILITARY MAYHEM

Lee Trevino once said that he played "World War II golf – out in 39 and back in 45." While that may get a chuckle, the folks at the St. Mellons Golf and Country Club in England were very serious about the war and posted the following rules:

Players are asked to collect bomb and shrapnel splinters found on the course.

In competition, during gunfire, or while bombs are falling, players may take shelter without penalty for ceasing play.

A ball moved by enemy action may be replaced, or if lost or destroyed, a ball may be dropped without penalty, not nearer the hole.

A player whose stroke is affected by the explosion of a bomb may play another ball under penalty of one stroke.

A guy goes to the doctor for a checkup. Afterwards, the doctors says, "I've got good news and bad news."

The guy says, "Give me the bad news first, Doc."

"You've got an incurable disease and probably won't live more than a year."

"Geez, what could possibly be the good news?"

"I broke 80 yesterday."

"Be honest, caddy" Weinstein said as he teed up his ball on the 18th hole. "Do you see any change in my game since we started?"

The caddy stroked his chin thoughtfully for a moment and replied, "Well sir, they're getting longer."

"My drives?" asked Weinstein.

"No, sir... our shadows."

Barney's on the 18th hole with two golf balls left, an old one and a new one. His tee shot has to go over a lake and he can't make up his mind which ball to play.

All of the sudden, the clouds part and a heavenly voice bellows, "Have faith. Play the new ball."

Barney can't believe his ears, but he's not about to doubt what he just heard, so he tees up the new ball. Once again, a voice from above roars, "Take a practice swing."

Barney scratches his head, but going along with the divine advice,

WHAT'S THE EASIEST GOLF STROKE?

takes his usual hacker's swing. Just as he's about to hit the ball, the clouds part one more time and the voice says, "Play the old ball!"

• • •

Manny, playing in a two-ball foursome, drove his tee shot to the edge of the green on a par three hole. Ralph, playing the second shot, managed to chip it over the green into a bunker.

Undaunted, Manny recovered with a fine shot to within three feet of the hole. Ralph missed the easy putt, leaving Manny to finish the hole.

"Do you realize we took five strokes on an easy par three?" said Manny.

"Yes, and don't forget who took three of them!" replied Ralph.

A TEE TOAST

May your balls, as they fly and whiz through the air,
Knock down the blue devils, dull sorrow and care.
May your health be preserved, with strength active and bold,
Long traverse the green, and forget to grow old.
　　　-From a letter written by Henry Callendar,
　　　Secretary of the Royal Blackheath Club
　　　(and also its captain in 1790, 1801 and 1807)

Irving and Irma were a loving, but very competitive couple. They also both talked in their sleep. Irving loved golf and Irma loved auctions. One night, in the wee small hours, Irving cried out, "Fore!"

Irma, deep in slumber, snorted and yelled, "Four-fifty!"

Father Flanagan was playing golf with a parishioner. On the first hole, he sliced his tee shot into the rough. His playing partner heard the priest mutter, "Hoover" under his breath.

On the second hole, his ball went straight into a water hazard. Again, the priest muttered, "Hoover."

He got lucky on the third hole as his tee shot landed on the green. "Praise be to God," exclaimed Father Flanagan.

He lined up his five-foot putt but missed it. "Hoover!" he yelled.

His opponent, now curious about the term, asked why the priest said "Hoover."

Father Flanagan responded, "It's the biggest dam I know."

"Never bet with a man named 'One-Iron.'"
-Tom Sharp

A pastor, doctor and car dealer were waiting one morning for a particularly slow foursome.

Finally, they became so tired of waiting, waiting and waiting that they sought out the greenskeeper.

The pastor said, "Hey, what's with that group ahead of us? They're slow as molasses."

The greenskeeper responded, "Oh, that's a group of blind firefighters. They lost their sight saving our clubhouse from a fire last year, so we always let them play for free whenever they'd like."

The pastor said, "That's so sad. I'll say a special prayer for them tonight."

The doctor chimed in, "And I'm going to contact my ophthalmologist buddy... Maybe he can do something for them."

The car dealer complained, "Why can't these guys play at night?"

WHAT A CARD!

After a pro-am at Doral in 1970, Raymond Floyd wrote his front-side score of 36 in the space reserved for the ninth hole. He signed the card and ended up with a round of 110.

The manager of the pro shop was confused about paying an invoice for some golf gear. Not exactly an Einstein at math, he asked his secretary for some help. "If I were to give you $15,000 minus 12%, how much would you take off?"

She answered, "Everything but my earrings."

GOLFER'S HOROSCOPE

Aquarius (Jan 20-Feb 18) **The Golf Club**
Born under the sign of the country club, you are industrious, prosperous and like to wear funny pants. Your idea of excitement is pulling the old "dead mouse in the golf bag" trick on the newest member of the club.

Pisces (Feb 19-Mar 20) **The Sand Trap**
You are a child of the sand trap. You are innately drawn to the rough and to water hazards. This is because in a former life, you were either Lewis or Clark.

> *"One of the nicer things about the Senior Tour is that we can take a cart and cooler. If your game is not going well, you can always have a picnic."*
> **-Lee Trevino**

Aries (Mar 21-Apr 19) **The Golf Tee**

Born under the sign of the tee, you came into the world along with the spring- which explains why the smell of newly mowed grass follows you everywhere. It's all those divots!

Taurus (Apr 20-May 20) **The Golf Ball**

Born under the sign of the golf ball, you tend to be round and dimpled all over.

Gemini (May 21-Jun 21) **The Golf Swing**

Like all Gemini golfers, you have a tendency to stand too close to the ball. Unfortunately, that's also true after you've hit it.

Cancer (Jun 22-Jul 22) **The 19th Hole**

The summer heat means that you are one of the chosen children of the 19th Hole. Trading golf balls for highballs, you play a round, then buy one.

Leo (Jul 23-Aug 22) **The Driving Range**

Your life is intimately tied up with the game. Sadly, the best drive you'll ever make is in a golf cart.

"Par is whatever I say it is. I've got one hole that's a par-23 and yesterday I damn near birdied the sucker!"
-Willie Nelson, on his personally built golf course

Virgo (Aug 23-Sep 22) **The Scorecard**

A Scorecardian, you are good with numbers...a talent you put to good use in cheating.

Libra (Sep 23-Oct 23) **The Water Hazard**

Under the sign of the water hazard, you are forever losing your ball in the drink. You have such an amazing ability at finding the water that your golfing companions refer to your woods as "diving sticks."

Scorpio (Oct 24-Nov 21) **The Golf Shoe**

You are tremendously gifted at golf. In fact, you immediately master any hole you attempt...especially the ones with windmills.

Sagittarius (Nov 22-Dec 21) **The Glove**

Though your tee time is late in the year, you are devoted to your sport. This is a shame because, basically, you stink!

Capricorn (Dec 22-Jan 19) **The Fairway**

Though you have much power, you are horribly inconsistent. In fact, you would do well to hit your first drive before deciding which course you'll be playing that day.

"If you want to meet new people, pick up the wrong golf ball."
-Jack Lemmon

PRACTICE MAKES PERFECT

When rain washed out the first two rounds of the 1983 Hong Kong Open, Greg Norman practiced by driving golf balls out the open window of his hotel room into the harbor. He won the tourney.

The word of the heroic deed had spread all over the country club. All the members were asking Irving about his Herculean effort in carrying his stricken partner back to the clubhouse for treatment.

"I can't believe Riley had a heart attack right in the middle of a game!" said one as he sipped his drink in the clubhouse.

"Yeah - and Riley must weigh what- 300 pounds? How did you ever manage to lift him over your shoulder and carry him back, Irving?"

"Well," said Irving, basking in the glory, "carrying him was nothing. It was picking him up and putting him down at every stroke that was the hard part."

An aggressive salesman was at a restaurant with an important customer when he spotted Arnold Palmer dining across the room. Aware that his client was a golf nut, he figured he'd try to score some points.

The salesman excused himself, went over to Palmer's table and said, "Pardon me, Mr. Palmer, but I've got a gigantic business deal in the works. My customer is a big fan of yours. If you'd stop by my table and just say, 'Hi, Joe,' this could put me over the top."

Palmer nodded his head and went back to his meal. When he finished, he went over to the salesman's table, tapped him on the back and said, "Hi, Joe."

Without looking up, the salesman snapped back, "Later, Arnie. Can't you see I'm eating?"

An expectant mother who was a couple of weeks overdue was told by her doctor to walk as much as possible every morning until the baby came. The M.D. also advised her husband that he should go along just in case anything started.

"Alright, Doc," replied the husband. "But would it be okay if she carries my clubs while she walks?"

"I like golf because you can be really terrible at it and not look much dorkier than anybody else."
-Dave Barry

Did you hear about the divorce lawyer who did a mailing to all the married male members of the exclusive country club?

She sent out 175 Valentines signed "Guess who?"

HOOKERS AND HOOKERS

Golf tournament organizers in Norco, California were arrested after police complained that prostitutes had been stationed at various areas on the course and were available to golfers between holes.

Two golfers are standing on the 10th tee. Jerry takes about 20 practice swings, changes his grip five or six times, and adjusts his stance just as much.

"Hey, Jerry! Play, for heaven's sake. We don't have all day," says Chris.

"Hold on a minute, I gotta do this right. See the woman standing up there on the clubhouse porch? That's my mother-in-law and I would like to get off the perfect shot," says Jerry.

Chris looks, and about 250 yards away he sees the woman. "You must be kidding. You couldn't possibly hit her from here."

THE BEAR IN THE AIR

Jack Nicklaus once used a helicopter instead of a golf cart as he played eighteen different holes on eighteen different golf courses in eight hours and forty minutes. He raised $590,000 for charity.

Harry the hacker was teeing off on the sixteenth hole of Pinehurst when he died of a sudden heart attack. The next thing you know, he stood before St. Peter at the Pearly Gates. "Welcome to heaven, Harry," said St. Peter. "Come, let me show you around the place."

St. Peter led Harry to a variety of beautiful places, including some of the best golf courses he'd ever laid eyes on. At one point, St. Peter brought Harry into a gigantic room with clocks all over the walls. "What are all these clocks for?" asked Harry.

St. Peter replied, "Ah, these are actually profanity dial indicators for all the golfers who've joined us this year. The more a golfer cussed on the links, the faster the hands move."

"Wow," said Harry. "Where's mine?"

"Sorry to report that they're using yours as a fan for the family room."

"Golf isn't a sport, it's men in bad pants walking."
-Rosie O'Donnell

Then there was the hunter who got a hole-in-one but went crazy trying to figure out how to mount it.

The guy was a first rate on-the-course and off-the-course louse. When he died, he went to Hell. His eternal punishment was to serve as a caddy for the Devil. This was not your normal golf bag toting duty. The Devil plays with a hot hand...oven-heated golf clubs and balls.

Just as the guy is prepared to caddy for the first time in Hell, he sees a former playing partner, a hideously ugly man, on the first tee with a beautiful woman.

The eternally damned caddy mutters out loud, "Why do I have to suffer like this when that guy gets to spend his time with a gorgeous woman like that?"

The Devil hears him and says, "Who do you think you are to question that woman's punishment?"

"One of the advantages of bowling over golf is that you seldom lose a bowling ball."
-Don Carter

TICKING OFF THE GOLF GODS

Arnold Palmer lost the 1967 Bing Crosby Pro-Am by virtue of the fact that his tee shot on the 14th at Pebble Beach hit a tree and bounced out of bounds. He re-teed and tried again, only to hit the same tree. Late that night, storm clouds gathered and a fierce Pacific gale uprooted the offending tree, ensuring that it would never bother Arnie again.

Sam and Moe were rocking on the porch of the palatial Miami country club after enjoying a round of golf.

Having talked about everything under the sun during their many games together, Sam was grasping for a new topic of conversation.

"Tell me, Moe, have you read Marx?" Sam asked.

"Why, yes," replied Moe. "And you know, I think it's the wicker chairs."

**WHAT'S THE OFFICIAL DRINK OF
THE NINETEENTH HOLE?**

A golfer's ball landed in a thicket of weeds in the middle of some woods, an unplayable lie if ever there was one. He tried to line it up but realized it was futile, so he picked the ball up and moved it to a better position, shouting to his playing partners, "Found it."

Suddenly, he had the feeling he was being watched. He turned around and saw an escaped convict whose picture had been plastered all over the newspaper.

The two men looked at each other for a long moment, and then the golfer whispered, "Shhhh. I won't tell if you don't."

THE WRONG CUP

Golf pro Homero Blancas, in the rough, carefully lined up his shot and then hit the ball. It bounced off a palm tree and landed in the bra of a spectator.

Blancas conferred with Chi Chi Rodriguez as to what he should do and Rodriguez replied, "I think you should play it."

LILAC CRAZY

Tom runs excitedly into the locker room and holds up a golf ball. "Look at this!" he says.

"Looks like a plain old golf ball to me," says Steve.

"This is no ordinary golf ball," Tom responds. "This is a golf ball that can not be lost."

Steve says, "Yeah, sure. Any ball can be lost."

"Not this one," replies Tom. "It's got a special radar tracking device so that if you hit it in the woods or rough or even the water, you can locate it."

"Oh yeah? Where'd you get this super-duper ball, anyway?"

"I found it."

Lonnie: I'll never play golf with my banker again.

Terry: Why not?

Lonnie: Every time I yell "Fore," he yells "Closure."

> *"You must expect anything in golf. A stranger comes through, he's keen for a game, he seems affable enough, and on the eighth fairway he turns out to be an idiot."*
> **-Alistair Cooke**

Harry was going by a large and deep bunker when he heard muffled cries for help. Peering down into the trap, he saw his buddy Larry trapped under an overturned golf cart.

"I think my leg is broken," groaned Larry.

"Does our lawyer know you're here?" called Harry.

"No, nobody does."

"Great," said Harry, climbing down into the trap. "Move over."

Two duffers were playing a round in Florida. The first one went off to find his ball in the rough while the second guy hopped in the cart and drove to the fairway. Minutes went by and there was no sign of the golfer in the rough, so his buddy hopped back in the cart to find his friend. He arrived on the scene to see his friend buried up to his waist in quicksand and sinking fast. "Stay still. I'll go get a rope to pull you out," said the second golfer.

"Forget about that! Quick - bring me a sand wedge!"

"It's still embarrassing. I asked my caddy for a sand wedge, and 10 minutes later he came back with a ham on rye."
-Chi Chi Rodriguez, talking about his accent

Four old golfers took to the links on a Saturday morning as they had every week for the past ten years. The competition was as keen as ever.

On the sixth hole, one of the golfers suddenly collapsed just as he was about to hit a bunker shot. As he lay on the ground, one of the other golfers shouted, "I think Nellie just had a stroke."

Said another player, "Well, just make sure he marks it on his card."

LINKS LUNACY

In 1954, Laddie Lukas shot an 87 at the Sandy Lodge Golf Course in England- a decent performance, but really extraordinary considering what he was wearing – a blindfold.

•

In Kansas City, Missouri there's a tournament called the Jim Smith Open. Who's it open to, you ask? Anyone named Jim Smith, of course. And yes, the trophy is engraved before the tournament.

WHAT DO YOU CALL IT WHEN A T-REX BREAKS EVEN IN GOLF?

The Bionic Invitational in Aiken, South Carolina is open to all those who've had a joint surgically replaced.

•

In 1962, an Australian meteorologist by the name of Nils Lied drove a golf ball a record of 2,640 yards, the equivalent of a mile and a half. How'd he do it? He was stationed at Mawson Base, Antarctica. His drive skidded along a sheet of ice.

•

Several decades ago, a Tournament of Champions was held in Las Vegas. Prize money was doled out in silver dollars.

TALK ABOUT POCKET POOL!

Sam Snead once drove a ball into the pocket of a man who was standing nearly 250 yards away. Unfortunately, the strict rules of golf called for Snead to play the ball where it lay. (And yes, we're just kidding.)

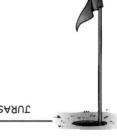

JURASSIC PAR

"Golf, golf, golf. That's all you ever think about," griped the newlywed bride at the dinner table. "You've been on the golf course every single day of our honeymoon."

"Sweetheart," cooed her husband in his most soothing tone as he reached across the table to take her hand. "Believe me, golf is the last thing on my mind at this moment. Now please stop this silliness and let's get back to our meal. Would you please pass the putter?"

A foreign spaceship hovered over a golf course and two aliens watched a lone duffer in amazement. The golfer hit his tee shot into the rough, took three shots to get back on the fairway, sliced the next one into the woods, and then took two to get back on the fairway again. Meanwhile, one alien told the other that he must be playing some sort of weird game, and they continued to watch in fascination.

The golfer then hit a shot into a bunker by the green. A few shots later, he finally made it onto the green. He four-putted to get into the hole. At this juncture, the other alien said to his partner, "Wow! Now he's in serious trouble!"

> *"The difference between a sand bunker and water is the*
> *difference between a car crash and an airplane crash.*
> *You have a chance of recovering from a car crash."*
> **-Bobby Jones**

Gale: Played golf with my boss the other day.

Howard: How'd it go?

Gale: Well, on the first hole, the boss topped the ball and only sent it about 20 feet, leaving it 375 yards from the hole.

Howard: What'd you do?

Gale: I conceded the putt.

Standing on the tee of a long par three, the confident golfer said to his caddy, "Looks like a four-wood and a putt to me."

The caddy handed him the four-wood, with which the golfer topped the ball about 15 yards in front of the tee. Immediately, the caddy handed him his putter and said, "And now for one heck of a putt."

HOW COULD HE MISS?
THERE ARE HOLES IN EVERY DIRECTION!

Alan Shepard became the first extraterrestrial golfer when he retrieved his smuggled 6-iron and package of balls from Apollo XIV in February, 1971 and took some practice shots on the moon. Even his poorest shot in the low gravity, airless environment of the lunar surface soared over 400 yards. As Shepard remarked with some satisfaction, "Not bad for a 6-iron!"

Then there was the bachelor who preferred golf to women. Even so, he finally found the love of his life and got married. You might say he learned to put his heart before the course.

Golfer: I think I'm going to drown myself in the lake.

Caddy: Think you can keep your head down that long?

Barrington: I say, did you hear what happened to Rockingham?

Hyde-White: No, I'm afraid I haven't.

Barrington: He was awakened in the middle of the night by a burglar and beat the miscreant into submission with a five-iron.

Hyde-White: Do tell. How many strokes?

"I'm glad we don't have to play in the shade."
-Bobby Jones, when told it was 105 degrees in the shade

Caddy: I'm terribly sorry, sir. I think we're lost.

Matty: Lost?! You told me you're the best caddy on the course.

Caddy: But we've been off the course for half an hour!

Bentley took a series of giant steps as he stepped out of the cart and made his way to the first green. "What the heck was that all about?" questioned his partner.

"Well," answered Bentley, "my wife told me that if I want to play tomorrow, it'll be over her dead body, so I'm practicing."

OUT ON A LIMB

In 1993, Germany's Bernhard Langer lodged a ball twenty feet up in a tree while playing in a tournament in England. Langer climbed the tree and knocked the ball out. Afterwards, when asked what club he had used, Langer responded, "A tree iron, of course."

One day on the links a man was separated from his companions for a few moments and the devil took the opportunity to appear to him. "Say, friend," the devil said with his best used car salesman smile, "how'd you like to make a hole-in-one to impress your buddies?"

"What's the catch?" asked the fellow suspiciously.

"It'll shorten your love life by five years," grinned the devil.

"Hmmm. All right, I'll do it," agreed the man.

He then went on to make one of the most spectacular shots ever and aced the hole. A few minutes later, the devil approached the man on the following tee. "How'd you like to go for two in a row?"

"At what cost?" asked the man.

"This'll shorten your love life by ten years."

"You drive a tough bargain, but okay," replied the golfer, who strode to the tee and sent a 310-yard beauty right into the cup.

At the next tee, the devil appeared once again. "This is a once in a lifetime offer. If you ace this one, it'll be three straight holes-in-one. It's never been done before in the history of the world. But it's gonna cost you another 20 years off your love life."

---

*"I like to say I was born on the nineteenth hole -
the only hole I ever parred."*
-George Low

"Let's go for it," said the man, who proceeded to dazzle everyone by hitting the ball from behind his back, sending it over a huge pond onto the green and right into the hole.

It was such an amazing shot that even the devil himself applauded. And that's how Father O'Malley got into the *Guinness Book of World Records*.

On the tenth hole, a foursome was getting ready to tee off when a man came running up to them completely out of breath.

"I say old chaps, I hate to interrupt, but I've just gotten word that my wife has fallen seriously ill."

"Bad break old boy," replied one of the men. "Is there anything at all we can do?"

"Well, if you don't mind, you could let me play through."

"I think I'll go cold turkey in the end and build golf courses. I'll torture other people."
-Irish golfer David Feherty, on what he plans to do after leaving the game

MANNY THE MAULER

In playing 18 holes in Riverside, California, Manny Neufeld
managed to hit fourteen spectators, two caddies and assorted
wildlife. Not satisfied with limiting his mayhem on the course, he
hit one ball over the fence, shattering the windshield of a vehicle
on an adjacent road and causing a six-car pileup. For his dubious
achievement, he received $10,000 to become a TV spokesman
for an insurance company.

Did you hear about the Siamese twins who wrote a book about
their golfing experiences? It's called *Tee for Two*.

They have some new equipment now that favors seniors. Like that
long putter you put right under your chin...You can putt and take
a nap at the same time.

WHY IS GOLF A LOT LIKE TAXES?

A duffer walks into the pro shop and says, "Pete, what can I do to lower my handicap?"

Pete the pro says, "Here, take this."

"But this is just a pencil."

"Yes, but it has an eraser attached."

BUSH LEAGUE

When one thinks of a wild and crazy practical joker, George H.W. Bush is not the name that usually comes to mind. Some might say the former president did have his moments – after all, he did pick Dan Quayle as his running mate. On one other occasion, he was playing golf with his National Security Advisor. In order to relieve the tension of his presidency, Bush, with the expert hands of a politician, pulled the old switcheroo on his golfing buddy and slipped him a trick ball. The ball exploded on contact. Bush got a good laugh, but the Secret Service was not amused!

YOU DRIVE VERY HARD TO GET TO THE GREEN,
ONLY TO WIND UP IN A HOLE.

Maybe you've heard about the duffer who's so bad, he has an unplayable lie when he tees up.

They're at the 19th Hole, watching the live telecast of the British Open when someone says, "Turn up the sound."

Someone else replies, "Ssssh...not while McIlroy is putting."

A guy applies for a sales position with a big golf equipment manufacturer. While he's waiting for the interview, the receptionist tells him, "You seem like a nice guy. Let me give you a tip. My boss is very sensitive about the fact that he doesn't have any ears. At some point, he's going to ask you if you notice anything odd about him. Whatever you do, don't make any mention of the ears."

The guy thanks the receptionist for the advice and goes in for the interview. Well, the boss is very impressed with the guy's resume,

---

"I wish my name was Tom Kite."
-Ian Baker-Finch, on signing autographs

his knowledge of the game in general and of golf gear in particular. But sure enough, at one point the boss says, "Tell me. Do you notice anything different about me?"

The guy looks at the boss and responds, "Well, now that you mention it, I can tell you're wearing contact lenses."

"That's amazing. I like perceptiveness in my employees. But how on earth did you know I wear contacts?"

"Easy. You'd be wearing glasses if you had any ears."

Terry and Joe were teeing off early one summer's day when the usual tranquility of the golf course was shattered by the siren of an ambulance racing to the maternity hospital atop a nearby hill.

"Somebody's getting a big surprise today," remarked Joe.

"I'll say," replied Terry as he lined up his putt. "When I left this morning, my wife's contractions were still at least an hour apart."

• • •

A very attractive but ill-intended young woman made it a practice to hang around the exclusive country club looking to settle down with a very rich and very old man. She found one in J.P. Fotheringham, the 92-year-old financier. Sure enough, she and J.P. tied the knot.

Within months, J.P. became ill. As his condition worsened, the old duffer was advised to make a new will. He asked his wife, "Honey, what should I do about my estate?"

She gently hugged him and cooed, "J.P., I think you should leave all of your worldly possessions to your greatest source of comfort."

Just a few days after his rewritten will was made, the old man died. At the reading of his will, his wife learned that he left 20 million dollars to his country club.

KNEE-JERK REACTION

Dave Ragaina was looking to win a bet. He used a 3-wood at a 207 yard, par-3 hole at a New Rochelle, New York course and made a hole-in-one. Oh yeah...he was standing on his knees at the time!

• • •

Taking some well deserved time off from their heavenly duties, Moses and St. Peter hit the links to indulge themselves in a game of golf. Moses teed up and hit a beautiful shot right down the fairway to the green, about two feet from the hole. St. Peter, however, whacked a bad hook which disappeared into the woods.

> *"Around the clubhouse they'll tell you even God has to practice his putting. In fact, even Nicklaus does."*
> **-Jim Murray**

Moses was smiling smugly when an eagle emerged from high over a nearby Interstate and dropped St. Peter's ball into the exhaust stack of a passing tractor-trailor. The pressure buildup soon shot the ball back into the air, where it was struck by lightning from some low-lying clouds. That sent the ball careening off a few chimneys, and it ricocheted right back to the golf course, landed on the green and rolled right into the hole. Moses sighed, turned to a smiling St. Peter and said, "Oh, c'mon- not when we're playing for money!"

Bismo the Gorilla was making a fortune for his owner. They'd travel around to golf courses and challenge the pro to a round of golf. They always accepted the bet, figuring that they could easily beat the muscle-bound primate- that was, until Bismo stepped up to the tee and drove the ball 450 yards. Then they'd usually give up, pay the bet and scamper away with their tails between their legs.

One morning, a top-rated country club pro conceded the bet after the gorilla drove the ball 450 yards to the green.

"Just out of curiosity," the pro asked as he forked over the cash, "how does Bismo putt?"

"The same as he drives," said the gorilla's owner. "450 yards."

> *"If you're stupid enough to whiff, you should be smart enough to forget it."*
> **-Arnold Palmer**

CATTLE DRIVES

In 1994, a German farmer sued the neighboring golf course over the demise of 30 of his cows after a veterinarian found a golf ball lodged in the throat of one of his herd. Further investigation showed that over 2,000 wayward golf balls had been gobbled up by the deceased cattle. In this instance, it was a case of the golfers keeping the farmer's head down.

Tiger Woods goes into the nineteenth hole and spots Stevie Wonder. "Hey, Stevie, it's Tiger. How's your singing career doing these days?"

"I can't complain. How are you hitting 'em?"

Woods responds, "My swing is going real well right now."

Stevie says, "Mine, too."

"What? You play golf?" asks Tiger.

"Sure ... I've been playing for years," replies Stevie.

WHAT TYPE OF ENGINE DO THEY USE IN GOLF CARTS?

"But you're blind," Woods says. "How can you possibly play?"

Wonder replies, "I get my caddy to stand in the middle of the fairway and holler to me. When I hear the sound of his voice, I play the ball toward him. Then, after I get to where the ball lands, the caddy moves down to the green and again I play the ball toward his voice."

"But how do you putt?" asks Tiger.

"Simple ... My caddy lies down in front of the hole and calls to me with his head on the ground. And then I play the ball toward his voice," explains Stevie.

"What's your handicap, Stevie?"

Stevie responds, "I'm a scratch golfer."

Woods says, "We've got to play a round sometime."

"Sure, but people don't take me seriously, so I only play for money - and never for less than $5,000 a hole."

"You're on. When would you like to play?" asks Woods.

Stevie says, "Pick a night."

FORE CYLINDER

The phone at the pro shop rang and was answered by the young clerk.

"These $300 shoes you sold me are too tight," complained the voice at the other end.

"Well, sir, for a shoe to fit properly, you have to make sure the tongue is pulled all the way out."

"Okay, but deth stilth feel awfulth tightth."

"Why do you keep looking at your watch?" the annoyed duffer asked his caddy.

"It's not a watch, sir. It's a compass."

• • •

How can you tell a bad golfer from a bad skydiver?

A bad golfer: *Whack!* "Oh, no!"
A bad skydiver: "Oh, no!" *Whack!*

"Two things that ain't long for this world - dogs that chase cars and professional golfers who chip for pars."
-Lee Trevino

THE WORLD ACCORDING TO CHI CHI

"Only in America can you explain a man working three days and making $52,500."

•

Rodriguez, on having reached a million dollars in career earnings: "The problem is, I'm already over $2 million in spending."

•

"I'm getting so old, I don't even buy green bananas anymore."

•

On the potential of an amateur: "I told him he was one year away from the Tour and next year he'll be two years away."

•

"Golf is the most fun you can have without taking your clothes off."

•

"When a man retires, his wife gets twice the husband but only half the income."

•

On his real name of Juan: "I think I'm going to change my name from Juan to Nine-Juan-Juan. I'm like the rescue squad. Whenever someone needs help, they call for me."

•

On the winds in Scotland: "The winds were blowing 50 mph and gusting to 70. I hit a par 3 with my hat."

*"I went to play golf and tried to shoot my age,
but I shot my weight instead."*
-Bob Hope

DUFFER-NITIONS

Graphite Shaft- what the guy who cheats on the scorecard gives you

Green- an area of smooth grass kept verdant and lush from years of constant sprinkling– usually by means of sobbing, whimpering and crying

Foursome- the best way to make slowpokes let you play through

Nineteenth hole- the only place related to the course where players don't worry about how many shots they take

Greenskeeper- the guy at the pro shop who keeps all your money

Driving range- what you want to make sure the hospital is within before playing golf with Gerald Ford

Dogleg- what you'll often see just before a water hazard

Fairway- that unfamiliar tract of closely cropped grass running from the tee to the green– otherwise known as that place your ball usually isn't

Duffer- a golfer whose actual score on any given hole is usually double his or her reported tally

> *"If you are caught out on a golf course during a storm and are afraid of lightning, hold up a 1-iron. Not even God can hit a 1-iron."*
> **-Lee Trevino**

A man tees up at the first hole. All of a sudden, a woman wearing a bridal gown comes running toward him. "You bum! You bum!" she screams.

"Aw, c'mon, dear," he says. "I told you only if it rains."

"Man, that Wally cheats," grumbled the golfer.

"Why do you say that?" his buddy asked.

"Today on the fourth hole, he lost his ball in the rough and slyly played a new one."

"How do you know?"

"Because I had his original ball in my pocket."

Of course you've heard about the foursome that was so bad they called themselves "The Bronchitis Brothers" because they were just a bunch of hackers.

"Golf is one of the few sports where a white man can dress like a black pimp."
-Robin Williams

CROQUET GOLF

Robert Jones made a pretty good shot at the Long Island Golf Course in 1951 with his ball landing nicely on the green, rolling to a stop 12 feet from the hole. The next player then hit a truly amazing drive– a drive that hit Jones' ball and knocked it into the cup. You might say he was really putt out!

Rodney was playing golf with a priest when a sudden storm blew up. The desperate pair found shelter in an old toolshed with a leaky roof, and as the lightning struck all around them, they saw a roaring tornado bearing down on the shed.

"Father," pleaded Rodney, "I don't want to die! Can't you do something about this?"

"Sorry," said the priest. "I'm in sales, not management."

HOW MANY GOLFERS DOES IT TAKE
TO SCREW IN A LIGHT BULB?

Golfer: "That can't be my ball. It looks far too old."

Caddy: "It's a long time since we started, sir."

This one comes from the star of *Caddyshack*, the man who got no respect, comedian Rodney Dangerfield: "Every time my wife takes the car, there's trouble. The other day, she came home, there were a hundred dents in the car. She said she took a shortcut through a driving range."

Bumper Snicker: If you think I'm a lousy driver, wait until you see me putt.

• • •

Then there was the dyslexic duffer who always wondered how to flog.

TWO- ONE TO DO IT AND ANOTHER TO TELL
HIM HE LOOKED UP

ODE TO THE 19TH HOLE

N is for nineteenth, the hole that's the best,
And the reason some golfers play all of the rest.
-From *Golf is a Four-Letter Word*, by Richard Armour

A golfer, playing one of the wilder courses in Alaska, was suddenly confronted by an angry grizzly bear.

"Oh, God! I'm doomed," he cried out.

Just then, a voice boomed out from above.

"This is God. You are not doomed, my son. You must smite the great bear on the nose with your fists."

Unflinchingly, the golfer obeyed and landed a few good roundhouse punches on the bear's snout.

"Now you must gouge out its eyes," God commanded.

The golfer reached up and forced his thumbs into the bear's eyes as hard as he could.

*"I play golf even though I hate it. I'm not done
with the game yet. I hate those windmills."*
-Mark Guido

"Now strike a great blow to the beast's head with your golf club," God instructed.

The golfer cracked the snarling bruin right between the eyes, causing the bear to rear up on its hind legs in a fury and bare its huge teeth.

"What now, God?" pleaded the golfer.

"Now, my son," God replied, "now you are doomed."

FLY BALL

Judy Rankin looked like she had the 1979, $150,000 LPGA Tournament locked up. She held a 5 shot lead after the 3rd round, but then things started to slip. It all came down to a critical putt on the 17th. Just as she drew her putter back, a fly landed on the ball. Some deep reflex in Rankin's brain must have signaled swat, because she whacked the ball so hard it went flying way past the hole, costing her the lead and the tournament.

> *"How come the white male politicians who vote against affirmative action are always so willing to accept a handicap on the golf course?"*
> **-Paul Krassner**

A guy was approached by a panhandler while walking down the street.

"Okay, if I give you money are you going to spend it on drinking?"

"No sir," came the quick reply.

"Will you gamble it away?"

"No sir."

"Will you use it to make bets at the golf course?"

"No sir. I don't play golf."

"Okay then. Come home with me for a few minutes and I'll give you a hundred dollars."

"A hundred dollars? Why do you want me to come home with you?"

"So my wife can see what happens to a man who doesn't drink, gamble or play golf."

What's the difference between a golfer and a fisherman?
When a golfer lies, he doesn't have to bring anything home to prove it.

"Golfers find it a very trying matter to turn at the waist, particularly if they have a lot of waist to turn."
-Harry Vardon

THE PITCHING GAME

In 1975, on the Port Royal Golf Course in Bermuda, Joe Flynn shot an 82, setting an eighteen-hole record for throwing the ball in a round of golf.

THE BEAR AND THE DOG

Jack Nicklaus relates this anecdote about a fellow he met at a dinner. The guy claimed his dog loved watching golf on television. He said, "The dog flips head over heels whenever you make a par and flips twice for a birdie."

Nicklaus asked him, "What does the dog do when I win?"

The man shrugged and said, "I don't know. I've only had the dog for five years."

An alligator was celebrating his 25th year of guarding a water hazard at a South Florida course. When the club pro asked him what he would like in honor of the occasion, the gator replied, "You know, I've always wanted one of those shirts with the little picture of Arnold Palmer on the front."

> *"The only problem with the Senior Tour is that when you're through here, they put you in a box."*
> **-J.C. Snead**

Poking around in the weeds for his ball, a handsome young golfer bumped into a beautiful young woman who was also seeking her lost ball.

"You know sweety, you look like my third husband," she purred.

"How many times have you been married?" he asked.

"Twice," she answered with a wink.

During a particularly crummy round of golf, the duffer sputtered to his caddy, "I'd move heaven and earth to break a hundred on this course."

"Try heaven," replied the caddy. "You've already moved most of the earth."

• • •

Caddy: Want a suggestion regarding your grip?

Duffer: How about around your throat?

WHY DID THE GOLFER WANT TO LIVE TO BE 125?

Three psychiatrists were at the nineteenth hole and got more than a little tipsy toasting each other's splendid play that day. The first psychiatrist says, "I have to admit something, something I'd only ever tell you two. I write prescriptions for drugs and get kickbacks for them. Not only that, but the kickbacks are under the table and I don't report them to the IRS."

The second psychiatrist says, "I have to admit something too. As you know, I have a lot of celebrity patients, and whenever one makes a juicy revelation in therapy, I sell the tip to the tabloids for big bucks."

After the two shrinks chuckle at all they're getting away with, they turn to the third and ask him what his deepest, darkest secret is.

"Well," the third psychiatrist replies, "No matter how hard I ever try, it seems I just can't keep a secret."

Bert: Hey, I just got a brand new set of golf clubs for my wife.

Ernie: Nice trade.

JUST ONCE HE WANTED TO BE ABLE TO SHOOT HIS AGE.

A REAGAN KENNEDY TICKET TO SUCCESS

Named after two presidents, is it any wonder that 6-year-old Reagan Kennedy likes golf? When she sank her 85-yard hole-in-one at a Central Illinois course in 2011 though, she was strangely silent. That might be because her dad always taught her never to make noise on a golf course. He didn't mention that the exception to the noise rule is whenever you make an ace. That's okay, because Reagan's older sister wised her up, and so a few holes later the younger Kennedy finally raised a celebratory ruckus. Oh, and forget that political moniker of hers. Republican or Democrat, the first grader with a hole-in-one under her belt has already proven to be non-'par'tisan.

Golfer: "Noticed any improvements in my game, caddy?"

Caddy: "Shined your clubs?"

Abe's ball landed in a deep ravine and as he flailed away trying to get it out, his golfing buddies heard "Whack! Whack! Whack! Whack! Whack! Whack! Whack!"

"Say Abe," his friend said when he finally emerged from the ravine, "just how many strokes was that?"

"Three," replied Abe.

"But we heard seven."

Abe managed to keep a straight face and replied, "Four of them were echoes."

At the Sleepy Hollow golf course, a foursome approached the 11th tee, where the fairway runs along the edge of the course and adjoins a highway. Forrester teed off and sliced the ball right over the fence. It hit the front tire of a bus and bounced back onto the green and into the cup for a hole-in-one.

"How on earth did you ever get it to bounce off that bus?" asked one of his astonished buddies.

"Well, first off," Forrester replied, "you've got to know the schedule."

"I deny allegations by Bob Hope that during my last game I hit an eagle, a birdie, an elk, and a moose."
-President Gerald Ford

A doctor and a lawyer met at the nineteenth hole after a round of golf. The doctor said, "How's your golf game these days?"

"I can't complain. I'm shooting in the mid-seventies," replied the lawyer.

"Honestly?" asked the doctor.

"What's that got to do with it?"

A guy just learning the game hired a professional golfer to play a round with him. After experiencing frustration after frustration on the links, the guy asked the pro, "What's my problem?"

The pro responded, "It's simple- you're standing too close to the ball ... after you hit it!"

A duffer lived a quarter mile from the local country club. One day he went into the pro shop and bought two dozen balls.

"You want these wrapped?" said the pro shop manager.

"Nah, I'll just drive them home."

"I'm an ordinary sort of fellow- 42 around the chest,
42 around the waist, 96 around the golf course,
and a nuisance around the house."
-Groucho Marx

McTavish looked out his window to see his neighbor MacIntire coming across the lawn.

"Ooooh how that man burns me," growled McTavish to himself. "He never comes over unless he wants to borrow something. Well he's not getting anything this time. Whatever he wants to borrow, I'll tell him I'm using it."

The doorbell rang, McTavish answered it and there stood MacIntire. Sure enough, without so much as a how-do-you-do, he said, "Say McTavish, I was wondering if you'll be using your lawn mower today..."

"I certainly will- and all day long to boot," McTavish replied firmly.

"Good," MacIntire smiled, "then you won't be needing your golf clubs."

BURROWING BALLS

A gopher in Winnipeg, Canada apparently had a hankering for taking golf balls from a neighboring golf course. The folks there found over 250 balls in the animal's nest.

> *"Golf scores are directly proportionate to the number of witnesses."*
> **-Anonymous**

A COSTLY BIRDIE

On a goodwill tour of South America, Sam Snead was about to hit
a bunker shot when he was unexpectedly attacked by an ostrich.
The bird was apparently interested in Snead's trademark straw hat.
When Snead put his hand up to protect his face, the ostrich bit it.
Slammin' Sammy was unable to play golf for two weeks.

TEE SHOTS
(Found on T-Shirts)
GOLFERSWHOTALKFASTSWINGFAST

I'M NOT OVER THE HILL
I'M JUST ON THE BACK NINE

I HATE GOLF
I HATE GOLF
"NICE SHOT"
I LOVE GOLF

GOLF SEPARATES THE MEN FROM THE POISE

**WHAT'S A HACKER'S FAVORITE
SOFT DRINK?**

STRIKES OR STROKES?

Baseball's Ted Williams and golfer Sam Snead once got into a discussion on which game was more difficult. Williams pointed out that, in golf, the ball isn't moving and it's hit off a flat surface. He added that he has to hit a ball flying at him at 100 miles per hour with a round bat. Snead thought about it for a minute and said, "Yeah, but you don't have to go into the stands and play your foul balls – golfers do!"

AND YOU THOUGHT YOU WERE BAD!

In 1985, *Golf Digest* sponsored a tournament which would determine the worst avid golfer in the U.S. The winner (or loser, more appropriately) was Angelo Spangola of Fayette City, Pennsylvania. On the 17th hole, a 138-yard par 3, Spagnola shot 66, hitting 27 balls into the water. He finished with a 257, 49 strokes more than the "runner-up."

Did you hear about the politically correct country club?

They don't refer to their golfers as having handicaps. Instead, they're "stroke challenged."

When a struck ball unintentionally veers to the left, it is known as a hook.

When a struck ball unintentionally veers to the right, it is known as a slice.

When a struck ball does not veer but instead flies straight forward, it is known as either a lie or a miracle.

A rabbi and a priest are playing a round with two others one day. One of the guys crosses himself before he tees off. The rabbi whispers to the priest, "What does that mean?"

The priest responds, "Not a thing if he can't play golf."

And then there's the one about the golfer who was so bad that in order to keep from going broke he had to start return addressing the ball.

WHAT DID THE ANCIENT ROMANS YELL ON THE GOLF COURSE?

TAKEN TO THE CLEANERS

Scotland's Raymond Russell was certain that he was going to finish up in one of the top 10 positions. However, going into the last round of the 2001 Compass English Open at the Marriott Forest of Arden, his hopes were, shall we say, sunk. At the 17th green, he threw his ball to the caddy for cleaning. The caddy missed the toss and was horrified as the ball rolled into the lake. The ball couldn't be found, resulting in a two-stroke penalty and 4,500 pounds in lost prize money!

A golfer at the nineteenth hole said to the bartender, "My good man, I find myself a bit short of cash at the moment, but I would love to have a drink to steady my nerves for my journey home."

"Sorry sir. No cash, no booze," was the gruff reply.

"Ah, but what about a wager? I'll bet you my golf bag here against a shot of your finest whiskey that I can show you something that will leave you totally amazed."

"Okay, you're on," said the bartender.

With that, the man took a gerbil out of his bag, gave it a tiny top hat and cane, and immediately the rodent went into a medley of George M. Cohan tunes. Dancing down the bar, the gerbil leapt to the piano and hopped from key to key, accompanying his own singing. Finishing up with a rousing *Give My Regards to Broadway*, the gerbil took a bow and hopped back into the golf bag. Slack-jawed, the bartender managed to mumble that it was truly the most amazing thing that he had ever seen.

The tattered old golfer knocked back his drink and then said, "Let's bet again – same terms."

As the bartender nodded in agreement, the golfer pulled a frog out of the golf bag and it began to croak *The Gettysburg Address*. A barfly noticed this and hollered, "Hey, I'll give you a thousand bucks for that frog."

The golfer said, "Sold," collected his money, and the man took off with the frog.

The bartender, while pouring another drink for the golfer, said, "I don't think that was so bright. A talking frog could be worth millions."

"Ah, don't worry about it," replied the golfer. "That frog doesn't talk. The gerbil's a ventriloquist."

"Pressure is playing for ten dollars when you don't have a dime in your pocket."
-Lee Trevino

THE LATE JOHNNY MCDERMOTT

Johnny McDermott, winner of the 1911 and 1912 U.S. Opens, traveled to Prestwick, Scotland in an attempt to qualify for the 1914 British Open. He arrived at Prestwick only to find that the qualifying rounds had been played the previous week.

ANIMAL ACT

When the Talamore Golf Course opened in 1991 in Pinehurst, North Carolina, golfers were offered the opportunity to purchase a llama as their caddy. The animals were capable of carrying two golf bags each and cost $200 per round.

"You think so much of your old golf game that you don't even remember when we were married," complained the pouting wife.

"Of course I do, Honey. It was the day I sank that thirty-foot putt."

> *"I'm hitting the woods just great, but I'm having a terrible time getting out of them."*
> **-Harry Toscano**

LIGHTNING BOLT

Tommy Bolt wasn't pleased with the caddy assigned to him for the day. He asked the tour official for a ruling when he said, "I know you can get a fine for throwing a club, but can you get fined for throwing your caddy?"

LIGHTNING BOLT II

Although Tommy Bolt was notorious for his temper, he will forever be remembered for passing gas at the 1959 Memphis Invitational Open. Just as his playing partner was about to putt, Tommy let loose. For his efforts, Tommy was fined $250 for unsportsmanlike conduct.

PRESIDENTIAL PARDON?

During a round at the Bannockburn golf course, President Woodrow Wilson's game was unexpectedly interrupted. Just as Wilson was about to hit a shot, a man ran onto the course and pulled the caddy off, grabbing him by the ear. As it turned out, Al Houghton, Wilson's caddy, was playing hooky from school, and it was his teacher who came to retrieve him. The president, however, convinced the teacher to allow Houghton to finish the round before returning to class.

Two duffers are downing a few at the nineteenth hole when one says to the other, "I'm taking my wife to the Holy Land to walk where the saints once walked."

The second duffer says, "Oh, you're taking her to Jerusalem?"

"Jerusalem? Heck no. I'm taking her to St. Andrews."

CHIP SHOTS

"Golf is a game in which the slowest people are in front of you, and the fastest are behind you."
-Anonymous

— • —

"The only shots you can be dead sure of are those you've had already."
-Byron Nelson

— • —

"Golf is good for the soul. You get so mad at yourself, you forget to hate your enemies."
-Will Rogers

— • —

"I own the erasers for all the miniature golf pencils."
-Steven Wright

— • —

"You make a lot of money in this game. Just ask my ex-wives. Both of them are so rich that neither of their husbands work."
-Lee Trevino

"Golf is a game invented by God to punish guys who retire early."
-Red Green

— • —

"Golf is a game where guts, stick-to-itiveness and blind devotion will always net you absolutely nothing but an ulcer."
-Tommy Bolt

— • —

"If I had cleared the trees and drove the green, it would've been a great shot."
-Sam Snead

— • —

"Ninety percent of the putts that fall short don't go in."
-Yogi Berra

— • —

"I have a tip which can take five strokes off anyone's golf game. It's called an eraser."
-Arnold Palmer

"Nobody ever looked up and saw a good shot."
-Don Herold

— • —

"Bob Hope has a beautiful short game. Unfortunately, it's off the tee."
-Jimmy Demaret

— • —

"Golf does strange things...
It makes liars out of honest men, cheats out of altruists,
cowards out of brave men and fools out of everybody."
-Milton Gross

— • —

"Columbus went around the world in 1492.
That isn't a lot of strokes when you consider the course."
-Lee Trevino

— • —

"When I told the career guidance person I wanted to be a golf professional,
he said that there's no such thing as a golf professional."
-Bernhard Langer

"Swing hard in case you hit it."
-Dan Marino

— • —

"I'm about five inches from being an outstanding golfer. That's the distance my left ear is from my right."
-Ben Crenshaw

— • —

"Golf is a game in which you yell fore, shoot six, and write down five."
-Paul Harvey

— • —

"I'd like to see the fairways more narrow. Then everybody would have to play from the rough, not just me."
-Seve Ballesteros

— • —

"Golf is an awkward set of bodily contortions designed to produce a graceful result."
-Tommy Armour

*"I'm not saying my golf game went bad, but if
I grew tomatoes, they'd come up sliced."*
-Lee Trevino

— • —

*"Some worship in churches, some in synagogues,
some on golf courses."*
-Adlai Stevenson

— • —

*"The best perks of this office are who you get to play golf with. I've played
with Jack Nicklaus, Arnold Palmer, Raymond Floyd, Amy Alcott."*
-President Bill Clinton

— • —

"Don't blame me. Blame the foursome ahead of me."
**-Football's Lawrence Taylor,
on why he was late for practice**

— • —

*"How did I four putt? I missed the hole.
I missed the hole. I missed the hole. I made it."*
-Fuzzy Zoeller

"A professional will tell you the amount of flex you need in the shaft of your club. The more the flex, the more strength you will need to break the thing over your knees."
-Stephen Baker

— • —

"The ideal build for a golfer would be strong hands, big forearms, thin neck, big thighs, and a flat chest. He'd look like Popeye."
-Gary Player

— • —

"The toughest hole is the nineteenth. I just can't get through it. It takes the longest time to play."
-Craig Stadler

— • —

"I went to bed and I was old and washed up. I woke up a rookie. What could be better?"
-Ray Floyd, on turning 50 and becoming eligible for the Senior Tour

— • —

"It's a marriage. If I had to choose between my wife and my putter — I'd miss her."
-Gary Player